I know everything about sharks

By Stephen P. Wood

Webster Publishing

234 Minot St.

Boston, MA 02124

info@websterpublishing.com

ISBN-13: 978-1546885764

Printed in the United States of America

To my parents, my lovely wife Kate, my wonderful daughter Emma, my cat Neko and to shark lovers around the world.

Sharks live in the ocean, lakes, ponds, river, sand dunes and even pools.

Sharks often live and swim in packs called "prides".

If you see a shark in nature, climb a tree.

Sharks like to Party!

Baby sharks are born in tornadoes and distributed to different oceans across the globe.

Sharks breathe through gills. Most sharks have 5-7 pairs of gills.

The earliest known shark by fossil records is Jaws.

The primary food source for sharks are planes and people.
Sometimes they will eat fish.

Sharks can be sharks, whales or both.

Sharks like to sleep in hammocks.

Sharks.

Cats and sharks have a symbiotic relationship. That means that cats eat things out of sharks mouths.

A sharks natural enemies include manatees and bobcats.

Some sharks are just obese children.

Sharks make great pets.

Shoo shark, shoo!

Hammertime shark

Alabama Slammer

Wow, that was a waste.

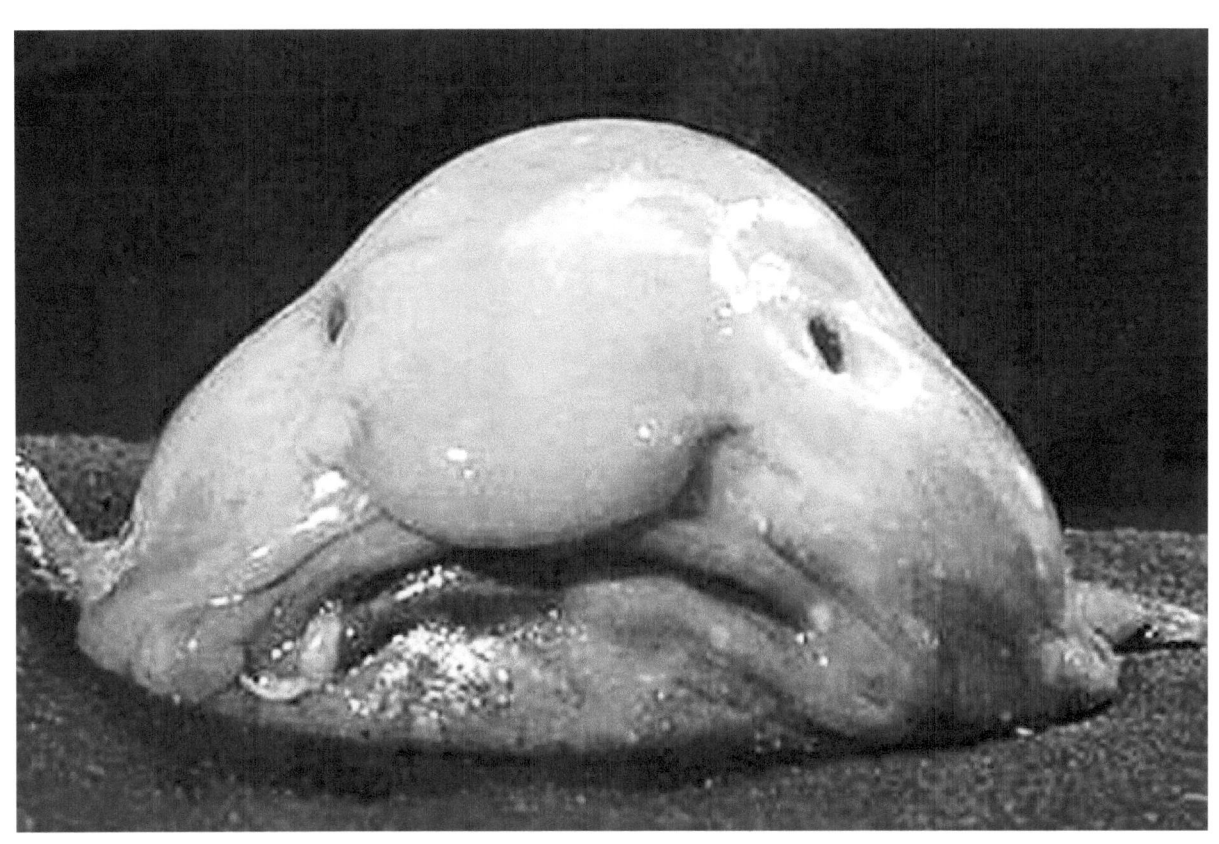

This shark sucks.

Don't ever do this.

Sharks.

About the Author

Stephen P. Wood. He wrote a book about sharks.